OR RECYCLE
recycled content

For Isatou and all who are "being the change" —M.P.

For all the crafters of the world —E.Z.

The author would like to thank Bill Roberts, Professor of Anthropology and Director of the PEACE program in the Gambia at St. Mary's College of Maryland, for his inspiration, guidance, and support. Further acknowledgments go to Isatou Ceesay and the many women of the Women Initiative the Gambia (WIG) who passionately shared their stories over the course of several visits. The author would also like to acknowledge her Wolof and Mandinka language tutor, Ebrima Colley, and the 2003–2008 US-Gambia Peace Corps education & environment staff who first introduced her to Isatou's grassroots efforts.

Text copyright © 2015 by Miranda Paul
Illustrations copyright © 2015 by Elizabeth Zunon

Back matter photos provided by Peggy Sedlak.

Millbrook Press
A division of Lerner Publishing Group, Inc.
241 First Avenue North
Minneapolis, MN 55401 USA

For reading levels and more information, look up this title at www.lernerbooks.com.

Main body text set in Oldbook ITC Std 17/24.
Typeface provided by International Typeface Corp.

Library of Congress Cataloging-in-Publication Data

Paul, Miranda, author.
    One plastic bag : Isatou Ceesay and the recycling women of the Gambia / by Miranda Paul ; illustrated by Elizabeth Zunon.
        pages   cm
    "Inspired by the true story of Isatou Ceesay and the recycling women of the Gambia"—Title page verso.
    ISBN: 978–1–4677–1608–6 (lib. bdg. : alk. paper)
    ISBN: 978–1–4677–6299–1 (EB pdf)
    1. Plastic bags—Africa, West—Juvenile literature. 2. Plastic bag craft—Africa, West—Juvenile literature. 3. Recycling (Waste, etc.)—Africa, West—Juvenile literature. 4. Pollution—Africa, West—Juvenile literature. 5. Ceesay, Isatou—Juvenile literature. 6. Wolof (African people)—Juvenile literature. I. Zunon, Elizabeth, illustrator. II. Title.
HD4485.A358P38 2015
363.72880966—dc23   2014009382

Manufactured in China
17 - 53484 - 13939 - 6/10/2022

ONE PLASTIC BAG

Isatou Ceesay and the Recycling Women of the Gambia

MIRANDA PAUL

ILLUSTRATIONS BY
ELIZABETH ZUNON

M MILLBROOK PRESS • MINNEAPOLIS

Njau, Gambia

Isatou walks with her chin frozen. Fat raindrops pelt her bare arms. Her face hides in the shadow of a palm-leaf basket, and her neck stings with every step.

Warm scents of burning wood and bubbling peanut stew drift past. Her village is close now. She lifts her nose to catch the smell.

The basket tips.

One fruit tumbles.

Then two.

Then ten.

The basket breaks.
Isatou kicks the dirt.

Something silky dances past her eyes, softening her anger. It moves like a flag, flapping in the wind, and settles under a tamarind tree. Isatou slides the strange fabric through her fingers and discovers it can carry things inside. She gathers her fruits in the bag.

The basket is useless now. She drops it, knowing
it will crumble and mix back in with the dirt.

Four goats greet Isatou as Grandmother Mbombeh emerges from her kitchen hut. "Hurry in before the rain soaks your beautiful *mbuba*!"

Isatou scurries in, and Grandmother serves spicy rice and fish. Rain drums on the creaking aluminum roof.

"I . . . broke your basket," Isatou confesses. "But I found this."

"Plastic," Grandmother frowns. "There's more in the city."

Day after day, Isatou watches neighbors tote their things in bright blue or black plastic bags. Children slurp water and *wanjo* from tiny holes poked in clear bags. Market trays fill with *minties* wrapped in rainbows of plastic.

The colors are beautiful, she thinks. She swings her bag high. The handle breaks.
    One paper escapes.
        Then two.
            Then ten.

Isatou shakes sand off her papers. Another plastic bag floats by, and she tucks her things inside.

The torn bag is useless now. She drops it to the dirt, as everyone does. There's nowhere else to put it.

Day after day, the bag she dropped is still there.
One plastic bag becomes two.
        Then ten.
                Then a hundred.
Plastic isn't beautiful anymore, she thinks. Her feet step
down a cleaner path, and the thought floats away.

Years pass and Isatou grows into a woman. She
barely notices the ugliness growing around her . . .

until the ugliness finds its way to her.

Isatou hears a goat crying and hurries toward Grandmother's house. Why is it tied up? Where are the other goats?

Inside, the butcher is speaking in a low voice.

"Many goats have been eating these," he says. "The bags twist around their insides, and the animals cannot survive. Now three of your goats and so many other goats in the village have died!"

Grandmother Mbombeh's powerful shoulders sag. Isatou must be strong and do something. But what?

Isatou's feet lead her to the old, ugly road. A pile
of garbage stands as wide as Grandmother's cooking
hut. Mosquitoes swarm near dirty pools of water
alongside the pile. Smoke from burning plastic stings
her nose. Her feet back away.

Goats scamper past. They forage through the trash for food. Her feet stop. She knows too much to ignore it now.

Holding her breath, she plucks one plastic bag from the pile.

Then two.

Then ten.

Then a hundred.

"What can we do?" Isatou asks her friends.
"Let's wash them," says Fatim, pulling out
omo soap. Maram grabs a bucket, and Incha
fetches water from the well. Peggy finds
clothespins, and they clip the washed bags
on the line.

As the bags dry, Isatou watches her sister crochet. "Can you teach me?"

"*Waaw*—yes." Her sister shows Isatou the stitches, then hands her a metal tool. Isatou's fingers busy themselves . . . in . . . out . . . around. "*Jerejef*—thank you."

Isatou finds a broomstick and carves her own tool from its wood.

"What's that for?" Fatim asks.

Isatou pauses. She and Peggy have an idea. But will their friends think it's crazy? Will the idea even work?

Nervously, she explains the plan.

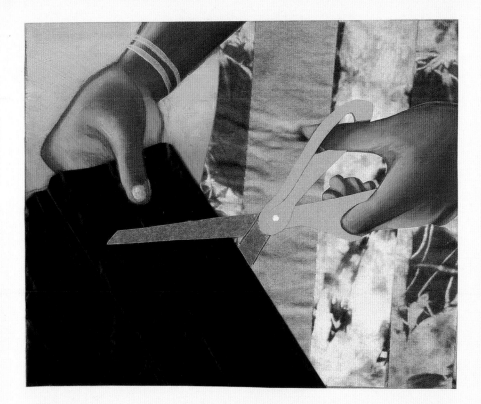

One friend agrees to help.
Then two.
Then five!
The women cut bags into
strips and roll them into spools of
plastic thread. Before long, they
teach themselves how to crochet
with this thread.

"*Naka ligey be?*" asks Grandmother. "How is the work?"

"*Ndanka, ndanka,*" answers Isatou. "Slow. Some people in the village laugh at us. Others call us 'dirty.' But I believe what we are doing is good."

The women crochet by candlelight, away from those who mock them . . .

until a morning comes when they will no longer work in secret.

Fingers sore and blistered, Isatou hauls
the recycled purses to the city.
One person laughs at her.
Then two.
Then ten.
Then . . .

One woman lays dalasi coins
on the table. She chooses a purse
and shows it to one friend.
    Then two.
        Then ten.
Soon everyone
wants one!

Isatou fills her own purse with dalasi. She
zips it shut and rides home to tell Grandmother
she has made enough to buy a new goat.

When she passes by the pile of rubbish,
she smiles because it is smaller now. She tells
herself, one day it will be gone and my home
will be beautiful.

And one day . . .

. . . it was.

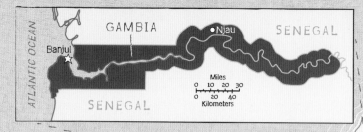

Author's Note

I first traveled to the Gambia, West Africa, in 2003 as a volunteer teacher. I had an amazing experience, but something threatened to ruin my memory of it all—the heaps of garbage piled everywhere.

The problem seemed too big to fix. Then a friend told me that in a rural village a woman named Isatou Ceesay was doing something about it. My friend showed me a beautiful purse made from recycled plastic bags, and I vowed to meet Isatou.

During my third stay in the Gambia, in 2007, I finally connected with Isatou and visited her home in Njau. There I interviewed many women and girls, including the original Gambian women who had begun the recycling project with Isatou a decade earlier. They shared past stories of dead livestock, strangled gardens, and malaria outbreaks linked to the trash. But they also shared new stories of healthier families, better income, and increased self-confidence. Although I wasn't able to include all the details about the women and their project in this book, I believe the story I've shaped captures their spirit and inspirational accomplishments.

Today, Njau is much cleaner, the goats are healthier, and the gardens grow better. Residents from nearby towns travel there to learn the craft of recycling. People from around the world continue to purchase the recycled plastic purses, and the women contribute some of their earnings toward an empowerment center where community members enjoy free health and literacy classes, as well as learn about the dangers of burning plastic trash.

In 2012, that center also became the home for the region's first public library. By the time you read this book, I hope that a copy of *One Plastic Bag* is shelved there and that it will be checked out once . . . then twice . . . then a hundred times!

Wolof Glossary and Pronunciation Guide

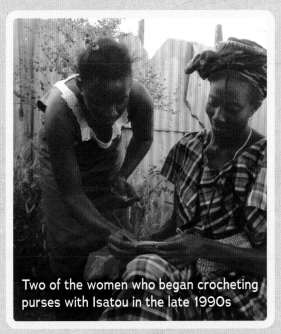

Two of the women who began crocheting purses with Isatou in the late 1990s

dalasi (duh-LAH-see): Gambian money

Fatim (FAH-teem): a Gambian girls' name and one of the original recycling women

Incha (IN-cha): a Gambian girls' name and one of the original recycling women

Isatou (EYE-suh-too): a Gambian girls' name and the first Gambian woman to recycle plastic bags

jerejef (jerr-uh-JEFF): thank you

Maram (MAH-ram): a Gambian girls' name and one of the original recycling women

Mbombeh (mBOHM-bay): a Gambian girls' name and one of the original recycling women

mbuba (mBOO-buh): a long dress

minties (MIN-tees): hard candies

Naka ligey be? (NAH-kuh lee-GAY bee): how is the work coming along?

ndanka, ndanka (nDAHN-kuh, nDAHN-kuh): very slow

omo (OH-mo): soap

waaw (WOW): yes

wanjo (WAHN-joe): a red drink made from hibiscus

Wolof (WUL-off): one of the native languages of the Gambia and the Senegal

Timeline

Women of Njau learn about the fair-trade movement (2007).

1970s Plastic bags become a serious problem in Gambian cities.

1972 Isatou Ceesay is born in Njau, Gambia.

1980s–1990s Plastic bags become a serious problem in villages such as Njau. Goats begin to die, and gardens struggle to grow in the trash-filled soil. Villagers burn their plastic trash to try to get rid of it.

1998 Isatou and Peace Corps volunteer Peggy Sedlak, along with four other Gambian women, begin the Njau Recycling and Income Generating Group (NRIGG). They work mostly in secret for over a year, until people become aware of the income and impact they are making.

2000 Isatou is named to the language & culture staff with the US Peace Corps in Gambia.

With donated funds, the women build a skills center, where they can work, learn, and form a community focused on better health for people, animals, and the environment.

2002 Isatou is promoted to assistant technical trainer for environment for the US Peace Corps in Gambia.

2005 Isatou is named an assistant field worker for women's empowerment with Future in Our Hands (a Swedish nonprofit organization).

Isatou and other NRIGG women begin to train people from nearby villages about the dangers of plastic and creative ways to reuse it.

2007 With nearly seventy women now active in NRIGG, the women of Njau begin marketing their products internationally.

2008 NRIGG wins a grant for sewing machines, and the women begin offering a tailoring/sewing workshop as well.

2011 Solar panels are installed at the NRIGG center, and the site is chosen to house the region's first public library.

2012 Isatou wins a World of Difference 100 Award from the International Alliance for Women (TIAW).

2014 NRIGG is incorporated as a registered nonprofit and is renamed Women Initiative the Gambia (WIG).

For Further Reading

Isatou Ceesay in 2014

Kamkwamba, William, and Bryan Mealer. *The Boy Who Harnessed the Wind.* New York: Dial, 2012.
This picture book tells the true story of a fourteen-year-old boy in Malawi who built a functioning windmill out of junkyard scraps in the face of a terrible drought.

McBrier, Page. *Beatrice's Goat.* New York: Atheneum, 2001.
Beatrice lives in a small Ugandan village and cannot afford to go to school. But when her family receives the gift of a goat, they sell the goat's milk to help her dream of attending school become a reality. The story is based on real events.

Millway, Katie Smith. *One Hen: How One Small Loan Made a Big Difference.* Tonawanda, NY: Kids Can Press, 2008.
In this story inspired by the life of Kwabena Darko, a boy named Kojo turns a small loan into the largest poultry farm in his region of Ghana.

Napoli, Donna Jo. *Mama Miti: Wangari Maathai and the Trees of Kenya.* New York: Paula Wiseman Books, 2010.
This book chronicles the work of Wangari Muta Maathai, the first African woman to win the Nobel Peace Prize, and her environmental efforts in Kenya.

Thompson, Laurie. *Emmanuel's Dream: The True Story of Emmanuel Ofosu Yeboah.* New York: Schwartz & Wade, 2015.
A picture book biography of Emmanuel Ofosu Yeboah, who bicycled across Ghana with only one leg, changing how his country treated people with disabilities.